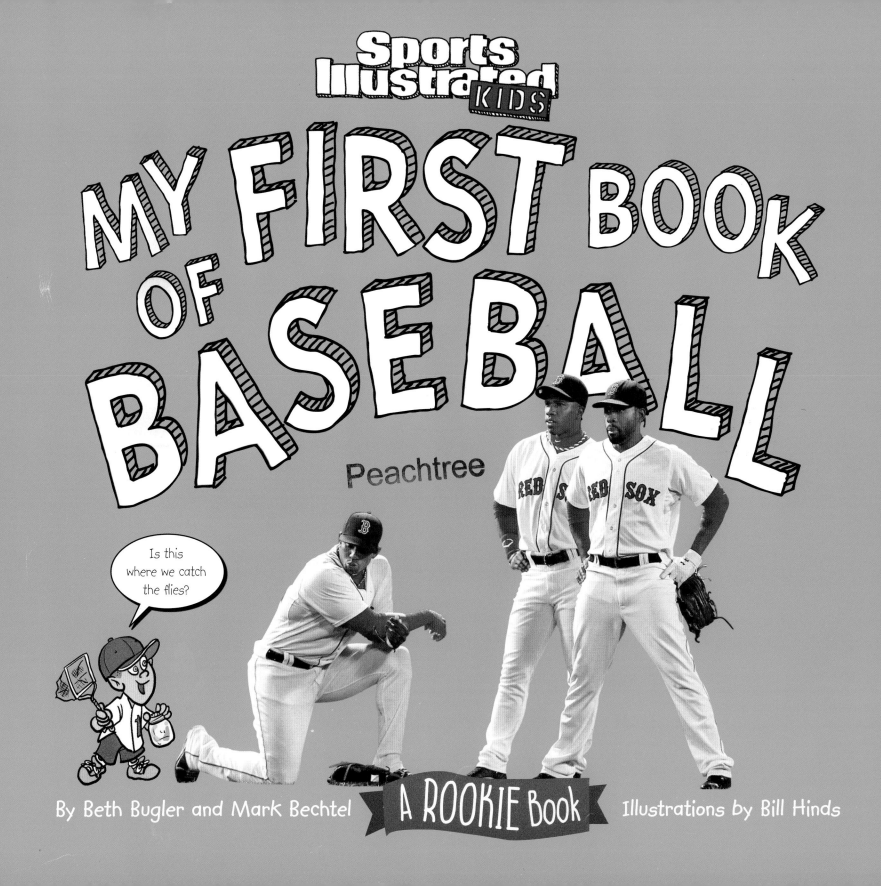

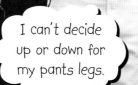

Baseball is a game between

TWO TEAMS.

Each team is made up of

NINE PLAYERS.

Unlike most sports, baseball has no running clock. Instead, the game is played for nine

INNINGS.

0:18

on't
this!

Each inning has two parts:

TOP OF THE INNING	The visiting team is on offense and the home team plays defense.
BOTTOM OF THE INNING	The home team is on offense and the visiting team plays defense.

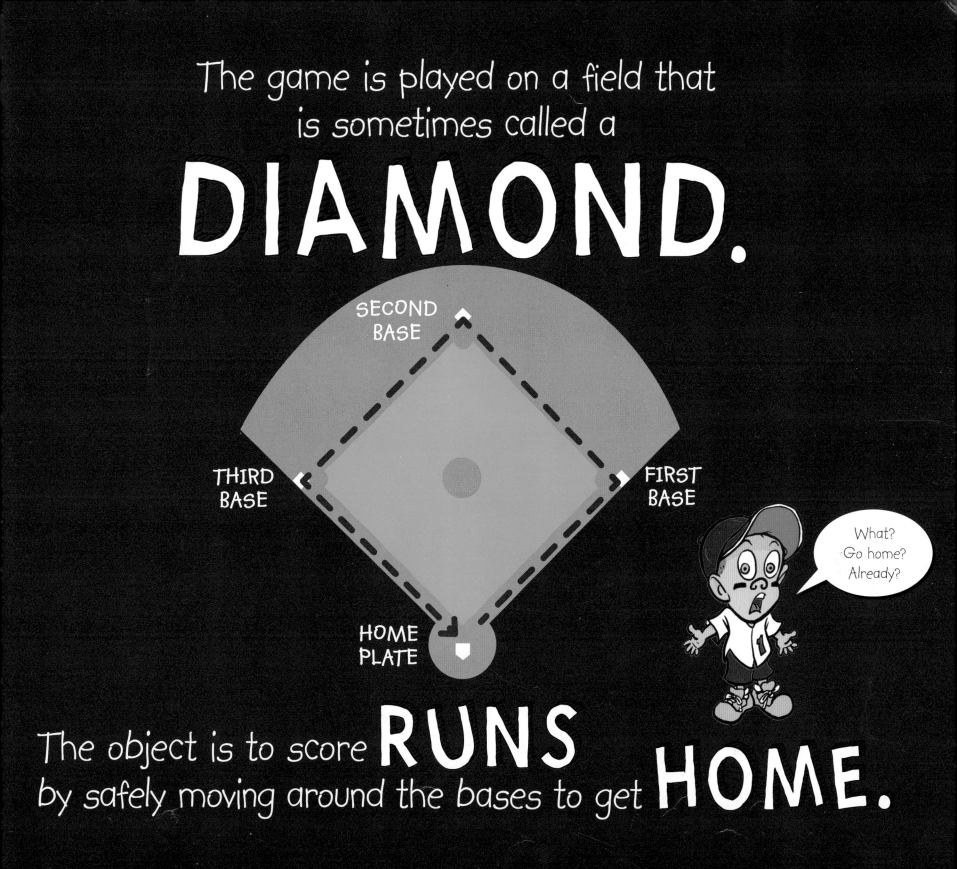

The guys with the bats are the

OFFENSE.

The players with the gloves are the

DEFENSE.

This is how the defense lines up in the

INFIELD and the OUTFIELD.

CENTERFIELDER

OUTFIELD

RIGHTFIELDER

LEFTFIELDER

SHORTSTOP

SECOND BASEMAN

INFIELD

THIRD BASEMAN

PITCHER

FIRST BASEMAN

CATCHER

I Know I usually hit third, but today I want to go first!

The first

BATTER

from the visiting team steps up to home plate.

Sixty feet, six inches away, the

The batter looks over at the third base coach.

They are each looking for a

SIGN

to tell them what to do.

VISITOR 0
HOME 0

And what are **YOU** looking at?

VISITOR 0
HOME 0

The batter

SWINGS,

and it's a . . .

FLY BALL!

The batter hits the ball high in the air. The defense tries to catch the ball before it hits the ground.

If you don't get it, I'm totally on it!

Got it! The batter is

OUT!

Three outs and the other team gets to come to bat.

It's a new inning and the batter hits a

GROUND BALL.

The ball rolls toward a fielder, who
tries to scoop it up and throw it to
first base before the batter gets there.

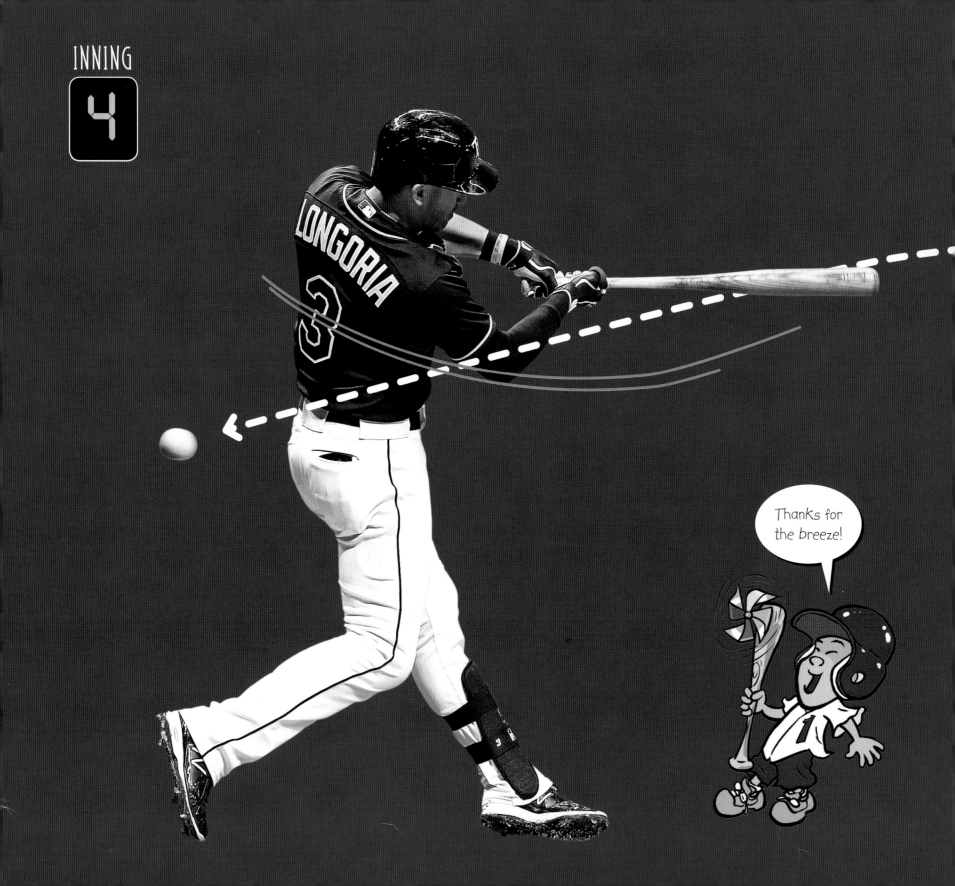

The pitcher throws the pitch.
The batter swings and misses.

STRIKE ONE!

Three strikes and you're out!

The pitcher tries to throw a ball that is hard to hit, but it must be in the

STRIKE ZONE.

- - - - - - - -

That's the area over home plate between the batter's knees and chest.

If the hitter doesn't swing at a pitch that's over the plate, it's a strike.

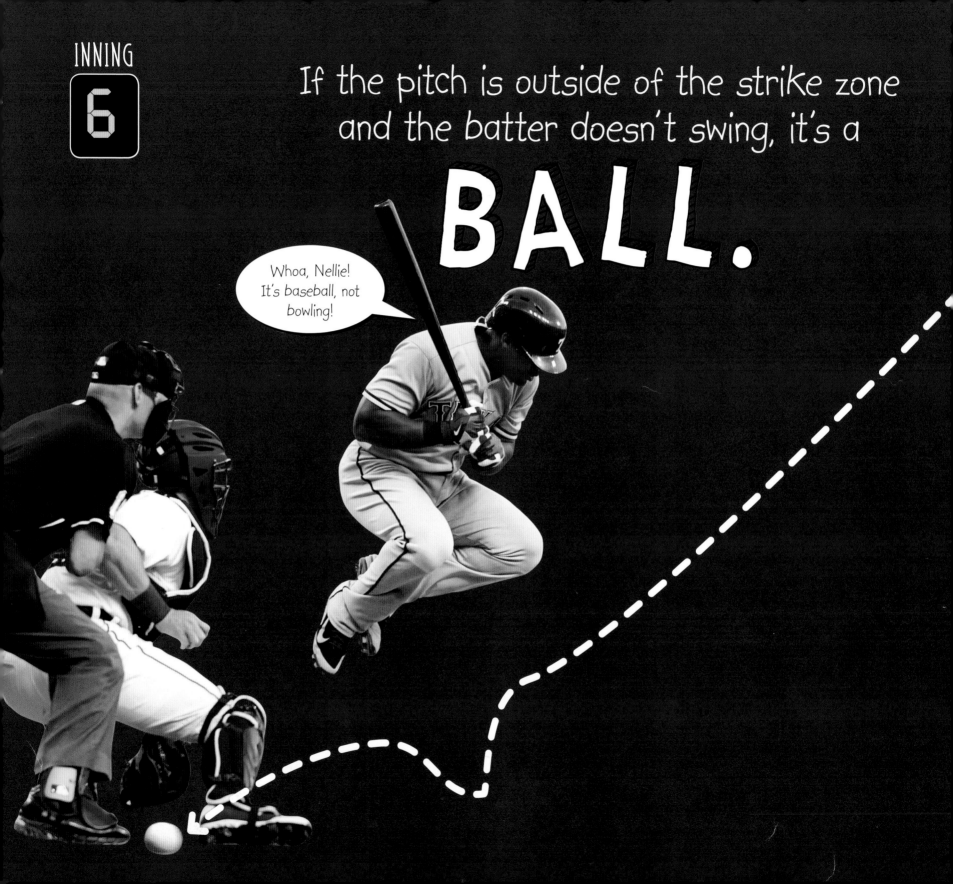

Four balls is a

WALK,

and the batter gets to go to first base.

Geez, slow down! It's called a walk, not a jog!

This hitter

CRUSHES

the ball, and everyone is off! The batter runs to first, the runner on first takes off for second, and the runner on second heads for third!

The defense tries to get the ball back to the infield as fast as it can.

You go there next.

Yay! The runner from second base makes it past third and crosses home plate. His team scores a

RUN!

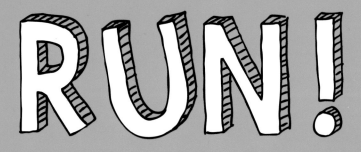

Thanks to my excellent directions!

. . . the runner from first base is trying to make it all the way to third. But the defense gets the ball to the third baseman, who

TAGS

the runner before he gets to the base.
He's out!

So . . . tag, you're not "it," you're "out!"

That's the end of the top of the seventh inning.
Since we've been at it for so long, it's time for the . . .

7TH INNING STRETCH

Stand up. Shake it out.
Sing "Take Me Out to the Ball Game,"
and take care of your business.

We're done stretching and
ready to get back to the action.
He swings and belts the ball . . .

The score is tied. The batter takes a big swing, but the ball doesn't go onto the field. It's a

FOUL BALL

because it's outside the foul lines.

FOUL LINE

MINE!

That counts as a **strike** — and the fan in the stands who caught the ball gets to keep it!

Now we're in the bottom of the ninth, and the game is still tied. The offense has a runner on every base.

Pants are feeling a bit tight. Too many nachos?

The BASES are LOADED.

The defense really needs an out. A run here means the home team will win the game. So the manager comes to the mound to talk strategy.

The manager decides that his pitcher is getting too tired, so he brings in a fresh, rested pitcher from the

BULLPEN.

I was three minutes away from a really good nap.

Wait, you were resting and not roping steer back there?

This is a huge moment. Can he get the big out?

No! The batter smacks the ball over the fence. **HOME RUN!** He scores, and the other three runners do, too. It's a

GRAND

It's time to celebrate!

Writers: Mark Bechtel, Beth Bugler
Designer: Beth Bugler
Illustrator: Bill Hinds
Production Manager: Hillary Leary

Copyright © 2016 Time Inc. Books

Published by Liberty Street, an imprint of Time Inc. Books
225 Liberty Street
New York, New York 10281

LIBERTY STREET and SPORTS ILLUSTRATED KIDS are
trademarks of Time Inc.

ISBN 10: 1-61893-167-9
ISBN 13: 978-1-61893-167-2
Library of Congress Control Number: 2015955030

First edition, 2016

1 TLF 16

10 9 8 7 6 5 4 3 2 1

Time Inc. Books products may be purchased for business
or promotional use. For information on bulk purchases,
please contact Ilene Schreider in the Special Sales
Department at (212) 522-3985.

To order Time Inc. Books Collector's Editions, please call
(800) 327-6388, Monday through Friday, 7 a.m.-9 p.m.,
Central Time.

We welcome your comments and suggestions about
Time Inc. Books. Please write to us at:
Time Inc. Books
Attention: Book Editors
P.O. Box 62310
Tampa, Florida 33662-2310

timeincbooks.com